LEADERS OF
ANCIENT EGYPT

CLEOPATRA | Ruling in
the Shadow
of Rome

LEADERS OF
ANCIENT EGYPT

CLEOPATRA

Ruling in the Shadow of Rome

Julian Morgan

the rosen publishing group's
rosen central

Published in 2003 by The Rosen Publishing Group, Inc.
29 East 21st Street, New York, NY 10010

First Edition

Library of Congress Cataloging-in-Publication Data

Morgan, Julian.
Cleopatra: ruling in the shadow of Rome / Julian
Morgan.— 1st ed.
    p. cm. — (Leaders of ancient Egypt)
ISBN 0-8239-3591-4 (library binding)
1. Cleopatra, Queen of Egypt, d. 30 B.C. 2. Egypt—
History—332–30 B.C. 3. Rome—History—Republic,
265–30 B.C. 4. Queens—Egypt—Biography.
I. Title. II. Series.
DT92.7 .M67 2003
932'.021'092—dc21

2002001214

Manufactured in the United States of America

CONTENTS

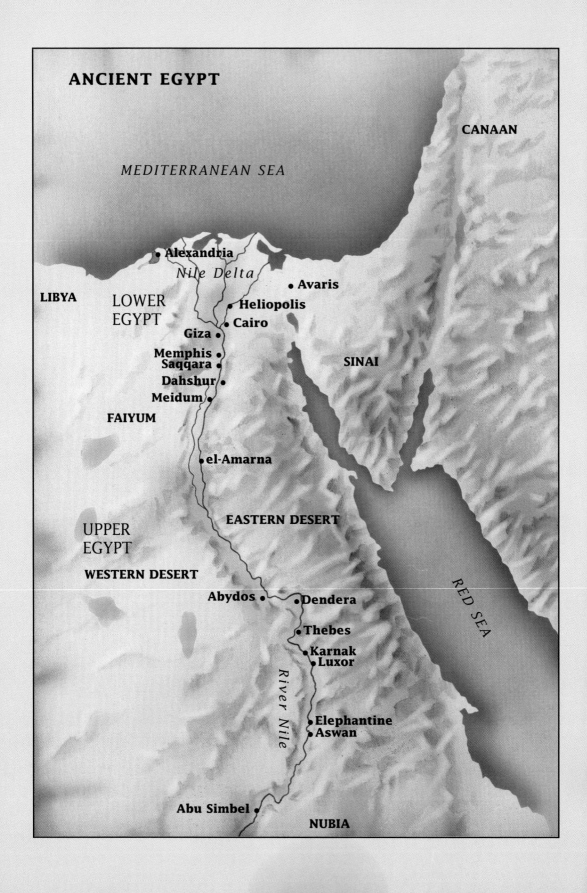

ANCIENT EGYPT

CANAAN

MEDITERRANEAN SEA

LIBYA

• Alexandria

Nile Delta

• Avaris

LOWER
EGYPT

• Heliopolis

• Cairo

Giza •

SINAI

Memphis •
Saqqara •

Dahshur •

Meidum •

FAIYUM

• el-Amarna

UPPER
EGYPT

EASTERN DESERT

WESTERN DESERT

RED SEA

Abydos • • Dendera

River Nile

• Thebes

• Karnak
• Luxor

• Elephantine
• Aswan

Abu Simbel •

NUBIA

THE EARLY YEARS

Alexander the Great of Macedon reached Egypt in 332 BC, when its history changed forever. He became the new pharaoh and was confirmed in his post by a royal oracle. A great new city was founded at the mouth of the Nile that bore his name: Alexandria. Macedonian Egypt was an important part of Alexander's swiftly expanding empire, but from this time on its rulers would be Greeks, not Egyptians. After Alexander died in 323 BC, his huge empire was split up into sections that could be more easily administered by local rulers. Egypt was awarded to Alexander's former general Ptolemy, and a new dynasty of pharaohs began.

The Greek Ptolemies would rule Egypt for the next 300 years, and the last of them would be

A Roman mosaic of Alexander the Great, who founded the Egyptian city of Alexandria

Cleopatra. She is often referred to as Cleopatra VII, as she was the seventh person with this name to have become queen of Egypt. In this account she will be referred to simply as Cleopatra.

Egypt at this time played a very important role in the Mediterranean economy. Each year the great river Nile, which flows from south to north across the country, was made to rise up by the melting snows of the mountains to the south, so that a huge flood, called the Inundation, took place.

The flood left a great deposit of mud and organic matter spread across the floor of the valley, and when the water levels finally receded the farmers could sow their crops in fertile new soil. Egypt's harvests were huge and its grain was exported across the known world, producing tremendous wealth for the Egyptians.

Cleopatra VII, queen of Egypt, as depicted by a Roman sculptor

Alexandria was a center for trade in glass, papyrus, wool, and other goods. The city had a medical school, a world famous library, and the Pharos lighthouse. Its architecture was much admired, and it was a cultural center without equal. Egypt's agricultural wealth and its industry made it a rich and powerful nation, but it still had to be administered carefully by its rulers, who controlled the production and the prices of many commodities.

The Ptolemies created a strong bureaucratic system of control across the land, and it became normal for the Greek rulers, wearing Macedonian felt hats and high boots, to treat the native Egyptian inhabitants as their slaves. Not one of the Greek kings or queens even bothered to learn the Egyptian language until Cleopatra came to rule. The land of Egypt suffered great internal strife, with a growing divide between Greek and Egyptian peoples, as well as between Alexandria and the rest of the country. The Ptolemies even employed eunuchs in top positions so that there would be no chance of them having their own successors. They kept themselves separate from their subject people, and adopted the ancient Egyptian royal custom of marrying their own brothers and sisters.

The early Ptolemies extended Egypt's territory to include the island of Cyprus, Cyrenaica (which occupied much of modern-day Libya), Syria, and Phoenicia. Further north, the Egyptians gained some cities and lands within Asia Minor and Greece, as their empire gradually grew in size. The first three kings, each called Ptolemy, were responsible for this, and it was only after the death of Ptolemy III in 222

BC that the empire began to decrease in size again. The early days of expansion were seen as a kind of golden age for the dynasty, which later rulers dreamed of recreating.

At the same time that Egypt's rule was contracting, however, the influence of Rome was growing in the central Mediterranean. The two states would have to learn to live together, though a natural mistrust existed between Greeks and Romans that would make this hard to achieve. The capture of Greece by Rome in 146 BC marked a time of change, as the Romans relentlessly came to control more and more of the lands around Italy.

In 80 BC, the Egyptians had a new king, Ptolemy XII, also called Ptolemy Auletes, meaning "the flute player." In typical fashion, he married his sister, Cleopatra V, and began a quest to establish an arrangement with the Romans that would secure his and Egypt's future. He had six children, of whom the first three were probably born to Cleopatra V and the last three to another wife. They were Cleopatra VI, Berenike IV, Cleopatra VII, Arsinoe IV, Ptolemy XIII, and Ptolemy XIV. Cleopatra VII was born in 70 or possibly 69 BC. Each one of these children was to become a ruler at some

This wall carving depicts Cleopatra as the goddess Isis.

stage in his or her life, and most of them met unfortunate deaths. This was a time of great change and disturbance.

EGYPT AND ROME

Rome wanted to control Egypt. As the Roman Empire began to grow in size, the number of mouths it had to feed also increased. Egyptian grain would help considerably, though if this could be secured without force or coercion, it would be a much more attractive arrangement.

The Roman general Pompey the Great had won several eastern lands for Rome in recent years, including much of Syria in 63 BC, previously controlled by another Macedonian dynasty, the Seleucids. He had also reduced the land of Judea to a dependent province of Rome, which had caused considerable resentment among the Jewish people living there.

By 60 BC, Pompey had formed an alliance, often called the first triumvirate, with two other leading Romans, Julius Caesar and Marcus Licinius Crassus. There were arguments for and against adding Egypt to Rome's growing empire, but for the time being it seemed best to leave it under its own control, especially if the local Egyptian rulers were pro-Roman.

Pompey the Great

Caesar had his eye on establishing a new province called Gaul in what is now France and Belgium, while the other two triumvirs kept a tight rein on the rest of the empire. It was felt that now was not the time to attack Egypt. Instead, the triumvirs agreed to accept the sum of 6,000 talents from Ptolemy XII, so that he could be recognized as a friend and ally of the Roman people.

The sum of 6,000 talents was a lot of money in those days. It is hard to say exactly how much in modern terms, but it has been suggested that it may have been almost all of the profits from one year's trading in Egypt.

Ptolemy XII, although keen to keep Roman support, was unable to pay the money in one transaction, so he borrowed it, knowing that he would have to repay it later from his country's revenues. He kept the loan quiet in Egypt, waiting for a good moment to tell his people. The money came from a Roman banker called Gaius Rabirius Postumus.

In 58 BC, the Romans decided to take over Cyprus. This island had been part of the Ptolemies' empire for over 200 years. It was governed at that time by the brother of Ptolemy XII, who committed suicide when he lost his kingdom. The loss of the island was keenly felt in Egypt, and the people were by now fully aware of the king's loan from Rabirius, as Ptolemy had raised taxes in order to start paying it off. As a consequence, Ptolemy fell from popular favor and had to leave Egypt suddenly. He went to Rome, possibly taking his daughter Cleopatra VII with him.

In the king's absence the new joint rulers of Egypt were his daughters Cleopatra VI and Berenike IV. This was customary, though in more normal times the joint rulers would consist of one male and one female member of the Ptolemy household.

Ptolemy XII found his claims for assistance in Rome well supported, as Rabirius put pressure on Pompey and Caesar to help restore him to his throne. If he was not returned to

Writing implements belonging to a Roman schoolboy

power, the money owed would not be repaid, so there were powerful arguments for supporting Ptolemy. His daughters, meanwhile, sought to accuse him of improper practices and sent 100 people to Rome to testify against him. Many of these witnesses were murdered as soon as they set foot in Italy, and the case against him was never presented. These acts demonstrate his ruthlessness as well as his ability to mobilize help in a foreign country.

As Ptolemy XII awaited an outcome, he left Rome and made his way eastward to Ephesus, on the west coast of modern Turkey. Here he made a deal with Aulus Gabinius, the governor of the new Roman province of Syria, who agreed to restore him to his throne by force in return for a fee of 10,000 talents. One of Gabinius's young officers, Mark Antony, persuaded him to accept the deal. This payment, combined with the earlier loan from Rabirius, would help secure Ptolemy's future. He knew that he would continue to receive support from Rome if he owed so much money to its people. Without his presence, the debt would not be repaid.

At this point, Cleopatra VI disappeared from the scene, though it is not known exactly why. Berenike IV needed a co-ruler, so she sought a husband. She first fixed on a man called Seleucus, probably from the fallen dynasty in Syria, but she was so disappointed in him that she ordered him to be strangled to death three days after he arrived in Alexandria. She then arranged a marriage with Archelaus, a prince from Pontus, the area south of the Black Sea. He had been a friend of Pompey the Great, supporting him on his campaigns and extending hospitality to his lieutenant Mark Antony.

However, Archelaus soon died when Gabinius led his forces into Egypt. Antony saw to it that his former host received an honorable burial, which may have been when he met Cleopatra for the first time, though their famous love affair did not spring up for many years to come.

In the meantime, his decent behavior probably earned him some popularity among the Alexandrians. Ptolemy XII was restored to his throne in 55 BC. Gabinius and Rabirius together tried to extract as much wealth from Egypt as they could, in return for their loans. They were both forced out of Egypt for their unreasonable conduct. Gabinius went into exile, and Rabirius received a pledge from Julius Caesar that he would get his money back for him. The army of Gabinius was retained by Ptolemy XII, who used it as a mercenary force in his own country. Berenike IV was killed on her father's orders for her treachery to him.

Ptolemy XII needed a co-ruler under the custom of his dynasty, and in 51 BC he chose his daughter Cleopatra VII, aged about nineteen. This was her first experience of rule and she may have shared it for only a short time with her father, who died later in the year. She took more than power from him, however. It is clear that throughout her own reign Cleopatra sought to restore to Egypt the former glory of the dynasty. She understood, as her father had understood, that in a world increasingly controlled by the Romans, the only way to achieve success and long-term stability in Egypt would be to have Rome as a supporting partner. Without Rome's help, Egypt would become just another name on its long and growing list of provinces. This was the legacy Ptolemy XII left to his daughter, whose very name, Cleopatra, meant "the one who brings glory to her father."

CAESAR'S WOMAN

After her father's death, giving consideration to the dynastic customs of the Ptolemies, Cleopatra agreed to share her power with her younger brother, the ten year old Ptolemy XIII. As a male, he had priority over her. As a minor, however, he had to be represented by a council of advisers. It seems clear that these advisers disagreed forcefully with Cleopatra on a good many issues, not the least of which was her desire to maintain Rome's support. It is clear that she left Alexandria at an early stage of her rule, when things got too hot to handle. The pharaohs in those days had to be crowned twice, by both their Egyptian and Greek subjects, as the two groups over which they ruled were so different in nature. Unlike some of her predecessors,

Cleopatra had taken the trouble to communicate with her Egyptian subjects and make friends beyond Alexandria, which meant that she had support beyond the Greek communities. This allowed her to rely on friends in the south of the country, called Upper Egypt, when disagreements broke out.

A bust of Julius Caesar, who met Cleopatra when he pursued Pompey the Great to Egypt

One source of major disagreement between Cleopatra and Ptolemy XIII's council occurred when the Roman governor of Syria, Marcus Calpurnius Bibulus, sent his two sons to Alexandria to ask for the assistance of the former army of Gabinius, which was still in the pay of the Ptolemies.

Bibulus was under attack by the Parthians, who threatened to overwhelm Syria, and the main issue for him was the defense of Roman

A wall carving of Ptolemy VIII and his co-ruler and wife, Cleopatra, making offerings to the gods

territory. His two sons were murdered, however, as the soldiers in Egypt had no desire to go to Syria or to help the Romans there, whose side they appear to have abandoned entirely. Cleopatra arrested the individuals responsible and sent them to Bibulus to deal with, who in turn sent them to Rome for justice at the hands of the Senate. This caused great resentment in Alexandria, and may have been the decisive moment in the split from Cleopatra's younger brother's supporters, who would have resented not only what happened, but the underlying reasons for it—that is, Cleopatra's policy of giving way to Rome.

There may have been other problems, too, as it is known that there were crop failures in 50 and 49 BC, and that Ptolemy's council issued a ban on the movement of grain between different parts of Egypt, perhaps in a move to block supplies to Cleopatra.

THE ROMAN CIVIL WAR

However, the problems of Egypt were minor in comparison to what was happening elsewhere. A great civil war was going on across the Roman world between the forces of Julius

Caesar and those of his former colleague, Pompey the Great. In early 49 BC, Cnaeus Pompeius, Pompey's son, came to ask for Egyptian help on his father's behalf in this struggle, and he was warmly received by Ptolemy's council, who gave him some 500 soldiers from the former army of Gabinius along with sixty ships. Furthermore, grain was sent to Pompey's base of operations in Dyrrhachium (modern Durazzo in Albania), and Pompey was chosen as Ptolemy XIII's guardian. The boy Ptolemy XIII became embroiled in a large-scale conflict on the side of the man who was destined to lose, while his sister, Cleopatra, had managed to avoid any kind of partisanship. She was probably in the territory of the Nabataean Arabs by now, in modern Jordan. She was probably working out how to raise support for herself in a bid to return to Alexandria, not realizing at the time that her best chance lay in the failure of her opponents at home to back the right contender.

After a major defeat at Pharsalus, Greece, in 48 BC, Pompey himself came to Egypt for support, since he had received such generous help there the previous year. However, instead of receiving help, he was murdered by Achillas, a Greek officer in the Egyptian army, and by Lucius Septimius, a member of the former army of Gabinius. They came to pick him up in a rowboat and stabbed him as he came on board. The reasons for the assassination are unclear, but the leading minister of Egypt, Pothinus, who had been chairman of Ptolemy's council of advisors, seems to have been responsible. Pothinus did not want to see the conflict between Pompey and Caesar continue on Egyptian soil, especially given the political problems between his young king and Cleopatra. A cowardly act of violence seemed a good way out for Egypt, though it would guarantee no future deals with Caesar himself, who was very much to be feared at that time.

Caesar came to Egypt not far behind Pompey. He arrived in Alexandria with ten ships and about 4,000 soldiers, a negligible force. He was given Pompey's head and signet ring on his arrival, which must surely have disgusted him. Indeed, it soon became obvious that he would find it hard to get along with Pothinus, Achillas, or Ptolemy XIII. Caesar had purchased the Egyptian debt from Rabirius, and now he wanted to see it paid back to him. He made a critical mistake on his arrival in the

The remains of the Temple of Hathor, built during the reign of the Ptolemy dynasty

city by wearing the robes of a Roman consul and having attendants carry the emblems of his authority. This caused the Alexandrians to riot against him. They were determined not to capitulate to the Roman oppressor, whoever he might be. Caesar met with Ptolemy XIII, and was perhaps surprised to see Cleopatra arrive in the palace at Alexandria at the same time. The story is that she was smuggled in by sea from the east and brought to Caesar in a roll of bedding, concealed from her brother's supporters. Caesar judged her more trustworthy than Ptolemy XIII or Pothinus, and they became lovers.

In the months that followed, Cleopatra saw Caesar as the potential savior for the dynasty of the Ptolemies and the only man with sufficient power in Rome to secure the future of her house. Caesar probably saw her as the only guarantee that the money loaned by Rabirius would ever be returned. He also recognized that Egypt and Rome could coexist within a carefully contrived framework. Caesar, like Mark Antony later on, saw that the Roman habit of crushing foreign rulers was not necessarily the best way to achieve political stability. He must also have been attracted to Cleopatra physically, and her reputation as a seducer of men must have been justified in part. We are told that she was not especially beautiful, but that she had considerable charm. There are no reasons at all to believe that she was promiscuous, as we know only of her love affairs with two men, Caesar and Antony. Certainly she was able to bewitch other men to some extent, and this must have been the result of her personality rather than her looks, if we can believe the accounts told at the time. In portraits of her it appears that she had a rather large, hooked nose, which might not have looked especially attractive. At the time of her relationship with Caesar she was probably twenty-two years old, and he was fifty-two.

When Ptolemy XIII first heard of Caesar's affair with his sister, he tore the diadem from his head and rushed out into the streets of Alexandria in a rage. Pothinus must have been similarly furious and the rioting in Alexandria continued. The Egyptian army was called back to the city, as Caesar sent for reinforcements from Syria and Asia Minor. He sent representatives to meet with Achillas, the Greek army commander, but they were killed. The palace where Caesar resided was held under siege as

An artist's conception of the interior of the Library of Alexandria, which burned down in 47 BC

he racked his brains to decide what to do next. He managed to bring the royal brother and sister together, keeping Ptolemy XIII under lock and key. Then he awarded Cyprus to the Egyptian family dynasty, appointing sister Arsinoe IV and brother Ptolemy XIV as its joint rulers. The island had been acquired by Rome ten years earlier. By giving it back to the Ptolemies, Caesar was attempting to gain some support in Egypt and to split up the Ptolemy brothers and sisters into manageable units.

Caesar now made a bold raid, attacking and destroying the Egyptian fleet in the great harbor at Alexandria. Cleopatra must have had mixed views about this, as she saw her ships go up in flames, but she continued to trust in her lover. She must have been even more concerned to see the flames spread to her famous library. Many rare books were destroyed in the flames, though it is unclear whether the library itself was burned or the area nearby, where books were awaiting transportation. Caesar made the Theater of Dionysus his center of operations and he gradually gained control of more and more areas of the city. The great Pharos lighthouse was taken from the rioters but Caesar was cut off on the causeway leading to it. From there he had to swim to his ships in order to escape.

Arsinoe IV had not been able to go to Cyprus yet, and now she escaped from the palace, causing further concern and more widespread rioting. Her minister, the eunuch Ganymedes, accompanied her to the rioters and she was proclaimed queen.

Pothinus, under house arrest in the palace, sent a message to Achillas indicating his support for Arsinoe IV, but this was intercepted, and Pothinus was killed on Caesar's orders. In the meantime, Achillas was killed too, probably by supporters of Ganymedes, who was his enemy. The lack of coordinated resistance among the Egyptians certainly helped Caesar's cause. He now proceeded to release Ptolemy XIII, who took over command of the rebellious forces from Ganymedes. In

March 47 BC, reinforcements for Caesar arrived under the leadership of Mithridates of Pergamum, a Roman-controlled city in Asia Minor. The troops included soldiers from Judea, whose people had hated Pompey and were therefore well disposed to help Caesar in his difficulties. The final battle took place outside the city and Caesar reentered Alexandria as a conqueror. Ptolemy XIII was drowned in the Nile.

CAESAR AND CLEOPATRA

At the end of the Alexandrian war, Caesar was more determined than ever to make a deal with Cleopatra to secure control of Egypt. He had struggled hard to win back Alexandria for his young mistress, and now he wanted to see the reward for those efforts. Cleopatra was pregnant, and Caesar must have thought about her having his son, who might one day rule Egypt. If this could happen, the future loyalty of Egypt to Rome would surely be guaranteed. Caesar knew that the great wealth of the country placed it in a unique category, and that it would be hard to find any potential governor in Rome honest enough to be entrusted with its administration. So he took various steps to secure the future for Cleopatra and her country. His vision was shared by the queen herself, who continued to promote peace with Rome, as her father had done before her.

It was at this time, 47 BC, that Caesar and Cleopatra went on a cruise up the river Nile together, though the exact details of this trip are hard to establish. It seems that the queen wanted to show Caesar her country, whereas he in turn wanted to be seen by the people with her, as the guarantor of their safety. This was more than just a simple cruise. Caesar took 400 ships with him. He made various settlements before leaving, which included the appointment of the twelve-year-old Ptolemy XIV as Cleopatra's co-ruler. This was certainly just a token gesture, as Cleopatra was clearly the person in charge and she wanted no further factional disputes or problems from advisory councils. Ptolemy was given full responsibility for Cyprus, and it may have been Cleopatra's intention to occupy him with the island to keep him out of her way. Arsinoe IV was shipped off to Rome under arrest.

Caesar now restored to Judea the status it had enjoyed before Pompey had made it a

Roman province, making it a client kingdom of Rome. This meant that it could keep its own ruler as its king, provided that the government complied with Rome's will. This restoration was a reward for the help Judea had provided to Caesar in overcoming the Alexandrian rioters. When he left Egypt in the summer of 47 BC, Caesar also left three of his legions behind as a security force, comprising about 15,000 men. The legions could protect Cleopatra and her family from any further problems that might arise from her people, or they could act as a restraining force if the Egyptians tried to go it alone. Caesar left an ex-slave called Rufio in charge of this force. It is odd that he did not leave someone with a more elevated rank in charge, but perhaps this is a reminder that he was afraid to entrust a command in Egypt to an ambitious Roman officer who could become corrupted by its wealth.

After Caesar's departure from Egypt, Cleopatra must have felt much more secure than at any moment since first becoming queen in 51 BC. She could now control her own land and her own destiny, though clearly she had chosen to follow Caesar's star. Her son was born later in 47 BC, and he was commonly

The ruins of the Forum Romanum, the political and administrative center of ancient Rome

known as Caesarion, meaning "little Caesar." Her own name for him was Ptolemy Caesar, which stressed his family connections to both Rome and Egypt. There was some dispute about his parentage, but it was generally accepted that he was Caesar's son in fact as well as in name.

Caesar went on to crush the last of Pompey's followers at the battle of Thapsus, in modern Tunisia, in April of 46 BC. He then returned to Rome to celebrate four triumphs (parades) in short succession. One celebrated the victory in the Alexandrian war, where Arsinoe IV was included in the parade, bound in chains. She was then sent off to Ephesus, in modern Turkey, to be held a virtual prisoner at the Temple of Artemis. Her advisor, Ganymedes, was also paraded before the Romans before being killed for his part in opposing Caesar. Cleopatra came to Rome shortly afterward, as it would not have looked good for her to witness the disgrace of her own countrymen in Caesar's triumph. She stayed in one of his houses on the Janiculum Hill, where she was an honored guest. Her son, Caesarion, came with her, though neither one could have been exactly welcomed by Caesar's wife,

A Roman mosaic showing waterfowl, crocodiles, and people along the banks of the Nile

Calpurnia. As tribute, Caesar had a golden statue of her placed in the Temple of Venus Genetrix (the symbolic mother of Rome) in a newly developed part of the Forum. This was a major mark of favor, conferring the status of a divinity on her in such a public place. Caesar was now emperor of Rome in all but name, though his official title was dictator, which he eventually adopted on a permanent basis. Before this, a dictator had been an elected official of the city, chosen to serve in times of crisis for a limited period of time, but Caesar had other ideas.

Later in the year 46 BC, Caesar went on a campaign to Spain. Cleopatra may have returned to Egypt. Caesar's return to Rome in the following year saw them reunited, however, though in his will at that time he made no mention of Cleopatra or his supposed natural son Caesarion. His own authority and position in Rome came into question as leading senators began to detest his arrogance and unconstitutional usurpation of power. Cleopatra's presence in the city probably did not help. There was gossip about Caesar's wife, and it seemed as if Caesar thought himself above the normal conventions of society. In the end, however, he was assassinated on March 15, 44 BC. He was regarded as a threat to the continued existence of the republic, the system of government that guaranteed free Roman citizens a voice in the rule of Rome.

More or less on the eve of departing on a new campaign to Parthia, an expedition that Cleopatra intended to fund from her untold Egyptian wealth, Caesar was killed on the steps of Pompey's Theater, stabbed by twenty-three conspirators. For Cleopatra this was the end of her stay in Rome, as she swiftly escaped from the backlash and the chaos that would inevitably follow the assassination.

DIONYSUS MEETS ISIS

CHAPTER 3

After Caesar's death, the Roman world was plunged into civil war once more as different contenders strove to gain and hold power. The formation of the second triumvirate in 43 BC was a central part of this struggle. The three members of this new ruling junta were Mark Antony, Octavian, and Marcus Aemilius Lepidus. These three men saw their opportunity to punish Caesar's assassins, led by Marcus Junius Brutus and Gaius Cassius Longinus, while each also sought to increase his own power at the expense of the others. Certainly none of them would be loyal to the others unless it suited his interests. Now Cleopatra had to play a waiting game to see who would triumph and who she should support. She chose to do this in Egypt, well out of harm's

A pavement mosaic showing a Roman garrison stationed on the Nile

way. It seemed to her that there were three people in the world who had a legitimate claim to Caesar's position, but it was hard to tell who had the best chance of claiming it. Mark Antony was one. He was a supremely capable general.

Then there was Octavian, named in Caesar's will as his main heir and already showing great promise politically. Finally, her own son Caesarion could claim direct descent from the dictator. One of Cleopatra's first actions when she had returned to Egypt was to engineer the death of her brother and co-ruler, Ptolemy XIV. By doing this she was able to elevate Caesarion, or Ptolemy Caesar as she called him, to the position of her co-ruler. Although he was still very much a child at the time, perhaps not even three years old, this boosted her hopes for the continuation of an independent Egypt, while ensuring that she could retain full control over the monarchy.

Cleopatra was approached by envoys from Caesar's assassin Cassius, who sought protection and support for his cause in the East. He had come to Syria when Publius Cornelius Dolabella had arrived to take control of the province as its new governor. Dolabella had been an officer of Caesar, and now he had to remove Cassius before taking up his new post. He too asked Cleopatra for help, and she was uncertain which way to turn. In the end she sent Caesar's three legions from Egypt to join Dolabella, but he lost his claim to Syria and the armies went over to Cassius. Thus, unwittingly, Cleopatra had helped the killers of Caesar. Pressure continued to build on her, as Cassius had some support among her people in Alexandria.

In Cyprus, too, her governor Serapion supported Cassius, and Cleopatra was worried that if she did not back Cassius, there might be a move to bring Arsinoe IV, her sister, out of her enforced retirement in Ephesus and back to the throne of Egypt. Yet she did not want to support the men who had killed her lover, and she must have been relieved when Cassius and Brutus met in Smyrna, modern Izmir on the west coast of Turkey. This took their war north, away from Egypt, and she decided now to back the side of the triumvirs Antony and Octavian, despite the fact that Serapion had gone over to Cassius's side. Cleopatra sailed from Alexandria with her fleet, but a combination of bad weather and personal sickness drove her back home before she could lend any concrete help.

The Battle of Philippi was fought in 42 BC in northern Greece, and it was here that Antony and Octavian destroyed the forces of Caesar's killers, Brutus and Cassius, who both committed suicide. It appeared that Cleopatra had backed the right side, and Rome officially recognized her joint rule with Caesarion in Egypt as the triumvirs' reward

Mark Antony, whose defeat by Octavian at the battle of Actium sealed Cleopatra's fate

for her support of Dolabella and themselves.

ANTONY AND CLEOPATRA

After the Battle of Philippi, Cleopatra awaited further developments from Rome. The arrangement between the triumvirs was that Octavian would look after matters in the western half of the empire, including Italy, whereas Mark Antony would take responsibility for the

These are the ruins of Ephesus, the city from which Mark Antony ruled the eastern part of the Roman empire after the defeat of Caesar's assassins at the battle of Philippi.

eastern half. In particular, Antony wanted to take up where Julius Caesar had left off, pursuing a campaign in the far eastern end of the empire against Parthia. This nation had caused difficulties many times previously in Rome's history, and Antony felt that there would be great glory in adding it to the list of Rome's client kingdoms.

Caesar had a special reason for wanting to go, however, which Antony felt he had inherited. Marcus Licinius Crassus, Caesar's colleague in the first triumvirate, had been dealt a crushing defeat there in 53 BC, at a place called Carrhae, modern Harran, Turkey, on the far side of the river Euphrates. The Roman conquest of Parthia was motivated in no small part by the desire for revenge for the humiliating defeat of Crassus.

Antony now made his way to Ephesus, in Asia Minor, where he addressed the issues of governing his half of the empire. There were loyalties to be secured and armies to be paid, while supporters of Brutus and Cassius had to be punished. He had spent much of his time in the East and knew well what was expected there. Many of the cities he governed were Greek in origin, and Antony knew that their

The remains of the library at Ephesus, where Mark Antony assumed the roles of various figures from Greek mythology

loyalty could be acquired in ways that would not necessarily bring results in the western half of the empire. At Ephesus, he was hailed as a new Dionysus by his Greek subjects, and he found that he rather enjoyed the idea of being divine. Dionysus was the Greek god of wine, celebration, and regeneration, and the bringer of joy. Antony liked his wine and certainly enjoyed parties, so this suited him well. Another role he assumed was that of Hercules, as he swaggered about in character, dressed up in a cloak with a long sword at his side.

Celebrations aside, however, Antony was making a serious assessment of how to conduct his campaign against Parthia, and Cleopatra soon came to his mind as someone who could help considerably. Egyptian finance would help, as would a reliable source of supplies of clothing and provisions from Alexandria. He sent an

The head of the goddess Aphrodite, by the Greek sculptor Praxiteles

officer and friend, Quintus Dellius, to summon her from Egypt, and in early 41 BC the meeting took place at Tarsus, in Cilicia. The queen did not come immediately, but when she did it was done in style.

After hearing of Antony's assumption of the character of Dionysus, Cleopatra dressed herself as Aphrodite, the Greek goddess of love, and she sailed in her barge up the river Cydnus to meet him. The rear section of the boat was covered in beaten gold, while purple sails flapped in the breeze. The rowers had oars of silver, which dipped in the water gracefully to the sound of flutes playing. Perfume wafted from the boat, as fans were used to cool the queen and spread the scents. Cleopatra herself lay back under a canopy of gold, while her attendants were dressed either as cupids, Aphrodite's children, or as the Graces. The mythological themes were entirely suggestive of what might come next. Antony was overwhelmed by his desire for the queen. Aphrodite had come to Dionysus.

The pharaohs of Egypt had been worshiped as divine for centuries, so it was entirely natural for Cleopatra to be seen as godlike. In ancient Egypt, many of the Greco-Roman gods were identified with local Egyptian gods and goddesses, so Dionysus was often

A Greek terra-cotta bust of the god of wine and ecstasy, Dionysus

regarded as equivalent to Osiris, the Egyptian god of rebirth. The Roman goddess Venus, or the Greek Aphrodite, was regarded as similar to Isis, a goddess whose worship in Egypt was extremely popular. Cleopatra represented herself as the personification of Isis on Earth to Antony's Osiris, in a way that her own people could appreciate and understand, too.

The meeting at Tarsus produced different results for Antony and Cleopatra. On the evening of their meeting she invited him to dinner, where he was utterly dazzled by the display of lighted torches and lamps. The banquet was wildly extravagant, the first of a series of such parties that would often go on until very late in the night. Antony's purpose was to find out whether Cleopatra had really supported Cassius's side in the civil war or not, and how she regarded events now. Would she give him the money to pay his troops and the other commodities he needed to bring off his Parthian campaign successfully? Could he rely on the cooperation of Egypt now that the three legions left to guard it by Caesar had gone? How could he secure the queen's long-term loyalty?

Cleopatra, in turn, saw her chance to stabilize things in Egypt. She demanded that Arsinoe IV, her sister in Ephesus, be killed, on the grounds that she might have helped

Cassius. Serapion, her disloyal governor in Cyprus, was to be killed, too. Cleopatra also became pregnant by Antony.

Antony agreed to accompany the queen back to Alexandria, to visit the city himself and to secure their arrangements, though he came as a private citizen so as not to offend the Alexandrians, as Caesar had done seven years before. It is doubtful whether Antony and Cleopatra really loved each other at this stage, though they certainly enjoyed each other's company and lived life to the fullest. But both knew what they were doing, and both had their own separate plans for the future. They continued to have wild and extravagant parties. One story tells of eight boars that were roasted for a party of only twelve people, just so the cooks could guarantee that the meat would be perfectly ready to be eaten when the revelers called for it. The two lovers suited each other well. Antony's crude and hilarious behavior was mirrored by the queen's seductive charm. We are told that she hunted with Antony and enjoyed his games of dice and his heavy drinking.

RULERS OF THE EAST

In early 40 BC, Antony heard of two Parthian invasions that had taken place in his provinces. The Parthian king's son Pacorus had led an attack against Syria, while a former Roman general called Quintus Labienus had marched against the province of Asia. Antony's own garrison in Syria had deserted him, so the need for him to attend in person was pressing.

There were also problems in Judea, where the Parthian invaders managed to overthrow the local ruler, Hyrcanus, after proceeding there from Syria. Antony moved swiftly to Asia, when more disturbing news came to him of a war in Italy that had been waged in his name but without his direct involvement. His brother, Lucius, and his wife, Fulvia, had stirred things up against Octavian, and a

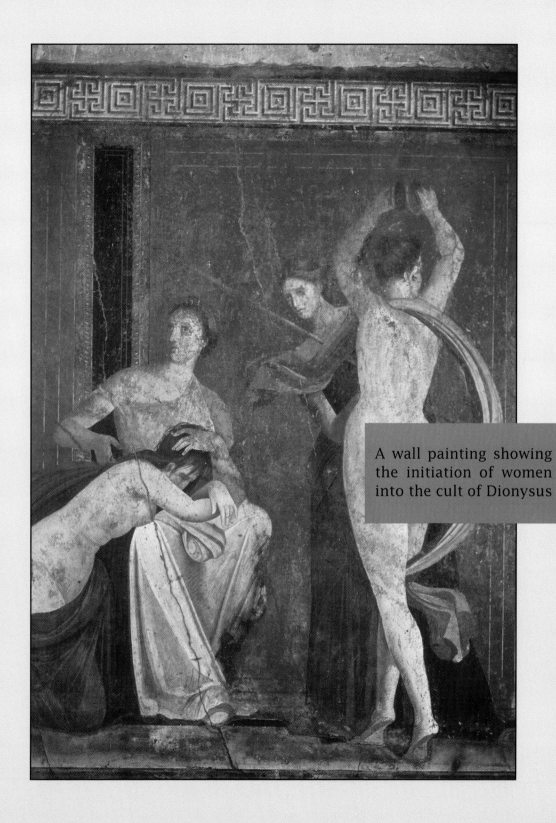

A wall painting showing the initiation of women into the cult of Dionysus

battle had been fought and lost in Perusia, modern Perugia in northern Italy. Antony knew that the problems in Italy were potentially more threatening to him than the Parthian menace, so he proceeded to meet with Fulvia, who had fled to Athens. He became very angry with her, and she died soon afterward of illness.

In October of 40 BC, Antony and Octavian met again at the port of Brundisium, modern Brindisi in southeast Italy, where they patched up the triumvirate and renegotiated their agreements. From this time on, Octavian would keep the Western empire, though Antony would be allowed to recruit soldiers in Italy, an important concession. Lepidus was given the province of Africa to govern, which roughly corresponds to modern-day Tunisia, and Antony was to continue to rule in the East, with a special commission to campaign in Parthia.

Lepidus was almost entirely sidelined now, and the triumvirate had become an arrangement between two major players, not three. However, the part of the agreement that would affect Cleopatra the most was the stipulation that Antony would marry Octavia, Octavian's sister. A marriage of convenience would secure the loyalty of both parties to the treaty, it was felt, and this would mean no more cavorting with the Egyptian queen.

Cleopatra must have been disappointed at this news. While she probably did not love Antony, she had just given birth to twins, his children, whom she had named Cleopatra and Alexander. She must have felt suddenly relieved when she heard of Fulvia's death, and perhaps a little optimistic that Antony would now return to her. The marriage with Octavia was a blow, therefore, and the pregnancy that followed cannot have been welcome news either. During this period the Parthian invaders had come right up to Cleopatra's borders, and she must have had this on her mind, though the Parthians did not at any point actually threaten Egypt.

Cleopatra was instrumental in helping the Judean prince, Herod, escape to Rome to ask for help, but when he returned she was annoyed that he had been confirmed as the single ruler in the province by the triumvirs. Cleopatra had cast jealous eyes on Judea. She continued to maintain that Caesarion was Caesar's true heir, though there was very little support elsewhere for this claim. News must

A Roman mosaic show-
ing a barge navigating
its way down the Nile

have reached her of Antony and Octavia's happy life together, their house in Athens, and the birth of their daughter Antonia, but she had no choice but to bide her time in Alexandria and wait for the next opportunity to present itself to her.

ANTONY AND OCTAVIAN

In the meantime, better news was coming from the East, where Antony's general, Publius Ventidius, was having some success in driving back the Parthian invaders. He managed to drive Labienus out of Asia and to his death, and Pacorus too was defeated and killed. Antony took troops as far as the Euphrates to consolidate these gains, which were celebrated in Rome. Then, however, Octavian called him back to Italy, to a second summit meeting at Brundisium. Antony attended the meeting, but Octavian did not, and the two men fell out again. Octavia helped to patch things up and another meeting was called, this time in Tarentum, modern Taranto in southern Italy. As a result of this meeting in 37 BC, Octavian promised Antony four legions of soldiers, 20,000 men, to help him in his

Parthian campaign. Antony gave 120 ships to Octavian so he could subdue Sextus Pompeius, a son of Pompey the Great, who had set up a base in opposition in Sicily. The triumvirate was renewed until the end of 33 BC, and the arrangements were secured by another promise of marriage, as Antyllus, Antony's eldest son by Fulvia, was betrothed to Octavian's daughter Julia. He was nine years old and she was seven, so this was a purely symbolic union.

After the Treaty of Tarentum, Antony returned to the East, but he sent Octavia, his wife, back to Italy. Within a short space of time he was in Antioch, Syria, where he sent for Cleopatra, whom he had not seen now for three and a half years. He seems to have realized that Octavian's promises were an illusion, and that the promised four legions would never actually arrive. He knew that Cleopatra could give him all the wealth he needed to raise armies in the East, and probably saw this as a better and quicker way to get on with things. It would be best if his wife Octavia could not see at close hand what he was up to, as his dealings with his former mistress were likely to involve more than just politics. Indeed, within a very short

The emperor Augustus, known in his youth as Octavian. His rivalry with Mark Antony eventually led to Cleopatra's defeat.

space of time the two were lovers again, though this time Cleopatra had managed to attach a set of conditions to her cooperation. We are told that she manipulated Antony by declaring extreme love for him. She ate so little that she wasted away, and she made sure that he saw her weeping. She did not want any chance of him returning to Octavia now.

All of her life, Cleopatra had sought the restoration of her family dynasty. The Ptolemies had ruled much of the coastal seaboard of the eastern Mediterranean, and she saw her chance now to recreate their old kingdom. The drawback was that she could only do this if the Romans gave the lands to her, as she had no intention at all of starting a military campaign. If Antony could promise her extended rule over his half of the Roman Empire, she in turn could regain the lost glories of her family. This was her condition for giving him what he needed, so he could achieve his aim of invading Parthia. By giving Cleopatra land, Antony felt that he was merely renegotiating how his portion of the empire was ruled, so from his point of view there was nothing improper in doing this.

Cleopatra was given much of Syria and Ituraea, including what is now Lebanon. She also received land in modern Jordan, close to Israel, as well as land in Cilicia, in southern Asia Minor. These gifts meant that much of the old dynastic empire of the Ptolemies was restored. Just as important, the lands in question were all heavily wooded, so the agreement was for Cleopatra to build enough ships to protect Antony's empire in the eastern Mediterranean.

Antony did not let her have it all her own way, however. Cleopatra very much desired the land of Judea and indeed probably regretted the help she had recently given to its king, Herod. Antony remained firm on this point, however, and Judea stayed in Herod's possession, though he had to surrender some of its coastline, including the port of Joppa. Herod's only port was now that of Gaza, and he also

This is another wall painting showing the initiation of women into the cult of Dionysus. This was a mystery cult associated with the pursuit of pleasure and ecstatic experience. Here a woman carries a plate of sacrificial offerings.

had to give up several date groves near Jericho, which he agreed to rent back from Cleopatra. The queen persuaded Antony to give her some of the land of the Nabataean Arabs in modern-day Jordan. She took ownership of the southern Dead Sea area, where bitumen occurred naturally in the water. Bitumen was a valuable substance used for a wide variety of purposes, including medicinal ones. Herod agreed to act as intermediary between her and the local inhabitants, which she agreed to, though perhaps she resented his involvement. A new relationship was in place between Egypt, the surrounding lands, and their Roman overlords. Cleopatra's children by Antony received new names at this time, marking the events. They were now called Alexander Helios (meaning "the Sun") and Cleopatra Selene (meaning "the Moon").

PATHWAYS TO RUIN

The situation in Parthia had changed during the last few years. A new king, Phraates IV, had taken over, having first apparently murdered his father and thirty of his brothers. He was entirely unafraid of Antony. Antony was finally ready to mount his campaign to expand Roman rule eastward. He moved north to Armenia and then south into Parthia, but here his plans went disastrously wrong. Phraates had organized a stiff resistance. Antony was forced to retreat, and on the retreat he was heavily attacked for twenty-seven days by the Parthians. He lost perhaps two-fifths of his entire army. By the end of the year 36 BC, he managed to reach a small village called Leuke Kom on the west coast of Asia Minor. Here he impatiently waited for Cleopatra to arrive. She brought money and clothing for his troops. Antony's major military failure had not prevented her from standing by his side, and she had with her his new baby, whom she called Ptolemy Philadelphus.

In spring of 35 BC, Octavian sent his sister to Athens to meet Antony and give him 2,000 men, as well as seventy ships. Clearly this was meant as an insult to Antony, as the original number of troops promised had been ten times this number, and the seventy ships were all that were left out of the 120 that Antony had first given to Octavian. Antony reacted bluntly, telling Octavia to go home. He accompanied Cleopatra to Alexandria, where she continued to try to change his mind about giving Judea to Herod. A friend of hers called Alexandra was the mother of High Priest Aristobulus, whom Herod had had killed, so Cleopatra demanded revenge. Antony called for Herod, heard his story, and decided to take no further action, though he did remove the port of Gaza from Herod's control.

Antony and Cleopatra continued to plan campaigns in the East, as King Artavasdes of Media promised support if they attacked Parthia again. First, however, Antony invaded Armenia again, with Cleopatra accompanying him as far as the river Euphrates. Antony's campaign was a success this time, and he brought great wealth back to Alexandria, where he intended to celebrate the victory in style. Cleopatra had taken a long route home, visiting her newly acquired lands, including Damascus in Syria. She called in to see Herod in Judea, which could hardly have been a friendly meeting.

In autumn of 34 BC, the couple were together again in Alexandria. Antony had the king of Armenia led in golden chains through the city in a procession to the Temple of Sarapis. He himself had taken up the role of Dionysus again, with his hair bound with ivy, riding in a special chariot and holding a sacred wand in his hand. Money and food were distributed in the streets in this extravagant ceremony, which was later called a triumph by Antony's enemy Octavian. In fact, it was no such thing, though certain parts of the event must have been very similar in style. The point of the accusation was that triumphs should only have been held in Rome, and only as part of a celebration held at the Temple of Jupiter. If this had been a triumph it would have been an illegal act, and one of terrible arrogance.

A painting of a victorious Roman athlete wearing laurels

THE DONATIONS OF ALEXANDRIA

Shortly afterward, however, Cleopatra and Antony held another ceremony, a great public affair in the Gymnasium at Alexandria. Seated on a raised silver platform, on golden thrones with their children below them, they made a series of pronouncements about their kingdoms. First Antony spoke about Caesar, and then proclaimed that he was dividing up the kingdoms of the Eastern empire. Caesarion, now aged thirteen, was Caesar's true son and would become king of kings, subordinate only to his mother, who would be queen of kings and queen of her sons, the kings. Alexander Helios, six, would become king of Armenia, Media, and all lands to the east all the way to India, which was taken to mean the Parthian lands that still had to be overcome. Cleopatra Selene, also six, was given Cyrenaica and Crete, while the baby, Ptolemy Philadelphus, two, became king of Syria, overlord of all the kings of Asia and king of the lands recently acquired by his mother. The whole event described here is normally referred to as the Donations of Alexandria, and it was to have dramatic consequences for both Antony and Cleopatra once their Roman enemies heard about it.

Cleopatra had wanted the Donations because they offered her a chance to establish exactly the kind of working relationship with Rome that she wanted. She was willing to pay the Roman armies and support Roman causes if the Ptolemy dynasty benefited from it. Like her father before her, she realized that the Romans were in charge and that Egypt could coexist with Rome only in a subordinate role, or it would be swallowed up into the giant empire. Her actions were later portrayed as threatening to Rome itself, as if she had some terrible ambition to rule from there.

In fact, Antony made it clear at all times that he was the supreme commander of Rome's eastern armies and that he would remain in control, no matter what else occurred. It is fairly certain that he loved Cleopatra deeply at this point, but his actions were not reckless. He saw shared rule by Greeks and Romans as a good model for stability in the region, and saw no need to insist on Roman dominance.

In spite of this, coins minted at this time show Marc Antony with his son Antyllus, making clear that his Roman child by his Roman wife Fulvia was still his real heir. This perception was important to him in Rome, where Octavian's supporters were busy trying to blacken his name.

After the Donations, Antony and Cleopatra resumed their turbulent life in the palace at Alexandria, where lavish extravagance was common. They were accused in Rome of drunkenness and perversion. Octavian accused them of adultery and lust, but in early 33 BC Antony wrote to him saying that this should come as no surprise, as Cleopatra was his wife.

This letter is very unclear in its content, as Antony knew well that he could not be legally married to Cleopatra for two reasons. First, he was married already, to Octavia, and second, Roman law would not recognize any marriage to a foreigner.

Antony went on to say that he knew full well that Octavian himself was enjoying adulterous relationships with other women, and he saw this as no crime, so it may be that his statement about his marriage to Cleopatra was meant in a sarcastic sense. It is hard to know whether he was or was not genuinely in love with the queen, but this does seem the best explanation for what happened afterward. Whether Cleopatra loved him is also hard to gauge, but her destiny was bound ever closer

A Roman wall carving showing a noblewoman eating while reclining on a couch, the typical fashion in which upper-class Romans dined

to him and it is hard to believe she did not love him, despite her ruthless ambition to protect her country and its people.

During the summer of 33 BC Octavian and Antony came into further conflict with each other as it became obvious that civil war was looming. Antony knew that with Cleopatra's wealth he could amass huge armies and that he was the more experienced general, with a long record of success behind him. He claimed that the victory at Philippi over Caesar's assassins had been his, and that Octavian had failed in the battle.

Antony repeated all kinds of slurs about Octavian, accusing him of failing to divide territories fairly with him, such as North Africa, taken from Lepidus, whom Octavian had demoted from the rank of triumvir without consultation. Octavian had behaved illegally with regard to himself as fellow triumvir and unconstitutionally at Rome, Antony claimed, failing to grant land for Antony's veteran soldiers to retire to in Italy.

In reply to this, Octavian launched a series of attacks on Antony and Cleopatra together. Antony was accused of sitting on a golden toilet seat, enslaved to the harlot queen whose design was to rule Rome. He would share North Africa when Antony shared Armenia.

Antony could give his soldiers retirement land where he had made new conquests. In the meantime, Octavian demanded, Antony should stop giving Roman lands away for foreigners to rule and start behaving like a Roman governor. Such charges and accusations were made before the final conflict. The Egyptian queen's name had become a byword for ambition, lust, and treachery in Octavian's propaganda campaign.

LOOMING CONFLICT

Antony had embarked on another campaign in the east, aiming to secure control over Media. But by October of 33 BC, it became clear that war was brewing in the west against Octavian. Antony returned to Ephesus and met Cleopatra there to prepare for war. He wrote to the senate in Rome offering to resign his position if Octavian would do the same, and asking for his actions in the east to be officially ratified by the senate.

At the start of the next year, 32 BC, the two consuls in Rome were both supporters of Antony, and it seemed for a while that he might succeed in his plans. During the first month of the year, however, the consul in Rome at the time was Gnaeus Domitius Ahenobarbus, who was too afraid to read Antony's requests out publicly in the Senate, as he thought that Cleopatra's name would damage the

Gold Roman earrings

A Roman wall carving showing children fighting

cause. Frightened off by Octavian's hate campaign, he left well enough alone until his colleague Gaius Sosius took the chair in February. Sosius proposed a motion of criticism of Octavian, but this was stopped by a tribune acting on Octavian's orders. The tribune produced written evidence showing that Antony was acting illegally.

In this way Octavian made it impossible for the Senate to carry on its duties. Three hundred senators left Rome and went over to Antony, while Octavian congratulated himself publicly for allowing them to leave in peace. This meant that there was no longer any effective political opposition to him in Rome. All of the parties involved had come to the point of no return, underlined a few months later when Antony divorced Octavia, the last link holding him to her brother and the last barrier between himself and Cleopatra.

After Antony's divorce from Octavia he too lost some of his supporters. Two men in particular changed sides and went over to Octavian in Rome: Marcus Titius and his uncle, Lucius Munatius Plancus. They had been friends of Cleopatra and staunch supporters of Antony up to this point. Why they

A painting from a tomb near Rome showing a ball game

changed sides is unclear, but they may have thought Antony and Cleopatra incapable of beating their enemy, or perhaps Cleopatra had insulted them.

On Plancus's return to Rome he spoke in hostile terms to the Senate about his former friends, and gave information to Octavian about Antony's will, which supposedly had been left in the Temple of Vest at Rome. Octavian then committed the highly illegal act of compelling the chief vestal virgin to hand over the will to him. He studied the will alone, and then made parts of it public. It said that Caesarion was indeed the true son of Julius Caesar, that Antony wanted his children by Cleopatra to inherit parts of his estate, and that he wanted on his death to be carried through the Forum in Rome before being taken to Alexandria for burial.

The first claim here was potentially damaging to Octavian as Caesar's heir, whereas the second claim indicated that Antony was living outside Roman law. The third claim, however, clearly showed that Antony saw himself as a man of the East. Octavian said that Antony was Cleopatra's puppet and that their shared design was to rule the empire from Alexandria, not

Rome. All these supposed claims were probably made up by Octavian, and even the will itself may have been invented. We will never know the truth of this.

Now the presence of Cleopatra began to disturb some of Antony's leading advisors. Gnaeus Domitius Ahenobarbus, who had feared to speak out against Octavian while consul in Rome, now urged his master repeatedly to send Cleopatra back to Egypt, as she was damaging to the Roman cause. She must have felt increasingly under attack and isolated, though Antony's general Publius Canidius Crassus took her side. Crassus said that she had as much right and more to be part of the force, and that she had wider experience of command than many of the others present. She continued to stick close to Antony, on whom she relied heavily. His loyalty was encouraged by her gift of 200 ships, 20,000 talents, and supplies.

In April of 32 BC, Antony and Cleopatra came to the Greek island of Samos, where they held a great festival in honor of Dionysus. The late-night parties and the wild festivities, together with the calling together of large numbers of actors from all across Greece, were yet one more lavish display of the Egyptian queen's

ATLANTIC OCEAN

GAUL

ETRURIA

ITALIA

CORSICA

Roma

Via A

ADRIAT

HISPANIA

SARDINIA

SICILI

Carthage

AFRICA

Boundaries of the Roman Empire ···················

THE ROMAN EMPIRE AT THE TIME OF CLEOPATRA

BLACK SEA

ARMENIA

PONTUS

Battle of
Philippi

MACEDONIA

ASIA

PARTHIA

Tarsus

ACHAEA

Nicopolis

Ephesus

CILICIA

SYRIA

Pharsalus

Battle of
Actium

CYPRUS

PHOENICIA

CRETA

JUDAEA

MEDITERRANEAN SEA

Alexandria

CYRENAICA

EGYPT

River Nile

RED SEA

wealth. Antony must have discussed invading Italy in order to catch Octavian unprepared, but she knew that her influence with him depended on the presence of her ships and her money, and she must have been reluctant to embark on a land war in Italy where she could not call the shots. He in his turn may have been afraid to march on his own country, knowing that this would make him widely unpopular.

After Samos they sailed west to Athens, where Gaius Geminus, a friend of Antony from Rome, came to tell him that he must rid himself of Cleopatra. She treated Geminus badly, even threatening torture, and he went on his way. Antony seemed too drunk to care. He summoned his son Antyllus from Rome, who would stay by his and Cleopatra's side in what was to come.

Octavian did not want to be accused of starting a civil war, so he declared war on Cleopatra, not on Antony, in the summer of 32 BC. The two lovers then took up their station at Patrae, modern Patras in Greece, as their forces were spread along the west coast of Greece. For some months there was considerable jostling, as Antony planned to block Octavian's ships on their way to Greece.

Octavian's leading general, Marcus Vipsanius Agrippa, assessed the situation and began to break down Antony's defenses one by one.

The final conflict occurred at the naval battle of Actium, which took place on September 2, 31 BC. After an indecisive struggle, Cleopatra retreated from the battle lines with her squadron of sixty ships. Her treasure was loaded on board, as were her sails, not normally carried by a ship going into battle. When she made her escape at full speed, Antony saw her leave and followed her. The presence of the treasure and the sails makes it clear that her escape was planned and was no simple act of cowardice. It must have been her intention to regroup her forces and fight again elsewhere, but if so, it proved to be the wrong decision.

Death in Alexandria

The clash at Actium was to some extent forced on Antony by Cleopatra's insistence that they should fight by sea, not by land, as his other generals urged. As they sailed south to Egypt he must have bitterly regretted ignoring the advice of his own people, and we are told that he sunk into a depression. News came to him that his huge land armies had been lost to him, persuaded to swap sides and join Octavian, although his general Canidius Crassus remained loyal and came to join him later.

When they both arrived in Egypt, Antony remained at the port of Paraetonium, on the border with Cyrenaica, in case Octavian might be behind him, while the queen made her way to Alexandria. On her arrival Cleopatra decked the bows

A view through the columns of the Temple of Horus, the falcon-headed Egyptian sky god

of her ships with trophies and pretended to have won a great victory, in case her people should rise up against her in protest for her losing the war. She had several leading Alexandrians killed, we are told, and hoarded together all the money and treasure she could, the best protection she could still muster.

When Antony returned to Alexandria, he lived for a short time alone near the Pharos lighthouse, staying out of Cleopatra's way. She may even have been grateful for this, as she knew she could easily lose the confidence of her own people now. After a short time, however, he left his retreat and rejoined the queen. They formed a drinking club called the Order of the Inseparable in Death and started on another round of late-night parties. Caesarion, now about sixteen, was enrolled into the list of adults, while Antyllus, Antony's son by Fulvia, was given the man's toga to wear for the first time. Cleopatra's co-ruler and Antony's heir were now both accepted as men, one of them Greek, the other Roman. Soon, however, Cleopatra began to fear for Caesarion's safety, and tried to send him away. She feared for her own future, too, and had a squadron of ships transported by land across the neck of land leading to the Red Sea, so she might escape from Egypt to the East. However, the Nabataean Arabs, the local inhabitants who had become hostile to Cleopatra and Antony when they were deprived of their right to collect bitumen on the Dead Sea, set fire to the ships before they could be used.

Octavian did not come immediately to Egypt, though his arrival there was clearly just a matter of time. Not only did Octavian need to crush his rival, he needed the wealth of Egypt to pay his soldiers. By the summer of 30 BC, he was present in Samos and Rhodes, where he confirmed the deal with Herod over Judea. Cleopatra had no allies left and her enemies were now all close to Octavian, who took up position at Ptolemais Ace. She felt the breath of disaster and sent a message to Octavian offering her abdication, provided that her children could rule in her place. Antony also sent a message to his enemy through his son Antyllus. Money was offered, and Antony said he would retire. Cleopatra offered more money. Octavian kept the money, but to all these approaches he remained impassive, knowing that he was on the point of complete victory. His only reaction to Cleopatra was an offer that he would agree to any reasonable terms if she had Antony exiled from Egypt or killed. He sent a messenger called Thyrsus to discuss terms with her, but Antony had him flogged.

Hearing that the enemy had taken the port of Pelusium, Cleopatra became enraged and commanded that the wife and children of its commander Seleucus should be put to death. She began to assemble all her valuables and treasure in her own mausoleum, together with firewood. She knew the monument could be sealed off, and the presence of the firewood might encourage Octavian to think twice before attacking her and watching her treasure go up in flames. As Octavian got nearer, Antony led a cavalry charge against the approaching troops and scored his final victory, successfully driving them back. Yet within days, by August 1, 30 BC, most of his soldiers had deserted him. This was the day that Octavian would later celebrate as the real moment of his victory. He even named the month of August after himself to commemorate the event, though this was years later, after he had first renamed himself Augustus. At a party late at night, Antony and his friends heard strange sounds, as if a group of partygoers were noisily leaving the city, going out through the

gate that led toward Octavian's troops. It was said by some that A carving of Hathor, the goddess of happiness and music

the sound was made by the gods who were leaving, abandoning Antony and Cleopatra.

A message came from the Mausoleum to Antony, saying that the queen was dead. This may have been just another part of the confusion that followed, or it may have been Cleopatra's deliberate attempt to drive Antony to suicide before trying to reach her own settlement with the conquering forces of Octavian. We cannot know the truth, but the effect on Antony was immediate. He stabbed himself in the chest with a dagger. As he lay dying he was brought to the Mausoleum, where his body had to be lifted up through a window. Cleopatra called him husband, lord, and emperor, and then gave him wine. Antony died and she set about embalming his body herself.

It is unclear how Cleopatra died herself, though various accounts say she may have met Octavian first. Did she try to captivate him, as she had done before with Caesar and Antony? This seems unlikely. She had beaten and torn at her hair and breasts in mourning for Antony, and her appearance must have indicated her grief. At thirty-nine years of age, she was older than the thirty-three-year-old Octavian, who loved his wife, Livia, and was in any case far too focused to let such a distraction affect his plans. He did not want responsibility for her death, but must have been delighted when he found out she had killed herself. Her attendants Iras and Charmian were found with her body, and the last words of Charmian were, "It is well done indeed and fitting for a princess descended of so many royal kings."

The story that she was killed by an asp, a type of snake, is just one of a set of stories sur-rounding her death. Modern scientists believe that a cobra may have been responsible rather than an asp, as her body was found in a state of peace that could have come about from that sort of poison. The cobra was often used by the pharaohs as a symbol of their power, and this would be a fitting end for a queen who had always sought to protect her dynasty in Egypt. Cleopatra's body was not disfigured, apart from some marks on her arms, and she wore her royal robes. Octavian exploited her death in a later

An Egyptian painted plaster mummy mask from the period of Roman rule

triumph, when a statue of her with a snake on it was paraded through the streets of Rome.

The queen's death marked the end of a remarkable life and the beginning of a new era for Egypt, which became a special sort of Roman province. It was too wealthy to be trusted to any

An ancient Roman cosmetics case

ambitious Roman senator, and future emperors retained it as a personal possession, governed by special envoys. Cleopatra was the last of the Ptolemies and the last of the pharaohs. She was a highly intelligent woman who had learned many languages so she could talk directly to her subjects. it is believed that she spoke Greek, Egyptian, Hebrew, Troglodyte, Arabian, Syrian, Median, and even Parthian. She always stayed faithful to her father's idea that

Egypt should be governed with Roman support, but now the West had prevailed over the East and her empire was vanquished. Her name would be blackened in the future by the man who had caused her the greatest damage in life, Octavian, who also controlled a propaganda machine that had systematically sought to destroy the good name of her lover Antony. Writers paid and supported by him described her as a deadly monster, a menace to freedom, her mind corrupted by drink and delusion. She was perverted, cruel, lustful, and arrogant, a byword for seduction in future generations. So they said. Cleopatra may have been some of these things, but for most of her extraordinary life she remained fully conscious of who she was—a queen.

AFTERMATH

Alexander Helios and Ptolemy Philadelphus were taken to Rome and were marched through the streets in Octavian's triumph. They were then taken with their sister, Cleopatra Selene, to Mauretania, in modern Morocco. Later Cleopatra Selene became the wife of King Juba II of Mauretania.

Antyllus sought protection in the large Temple of Caesar in Alexandria, after his father Marc Antony's death. Octavian was afraid to let him live, however, in case Antony's supporters should use him later on as the focus for a rebellion. He was beheaded, betrayed by his own tutor, Theodorus.

Caesarion was caught trying to escape from Egypt and was killed, as Octavian feared his connection to Caesar and how this might encourage later supporters in Rome or Egypt to use him as a figurehead for a future rebellion.

The general Marcus Vipsanius Agrippa continued to serve Octavian for many years to come. He was considered the finest general of his day and he married Octavian's daughter Julia. He died in 12 BC.

Octavian became the first citizen of Rome after his final defeat of Antony and Cleopatra. In practice, this meant that he became the first of the emperors, establishing his constitutional authority in settlements reached in 27 BC and 23 BC. He adopted the name of Augustus, meaning the "respected one." He reigned successfully until his death in AD 14.

HOW DO WE KNOW?

Primary sources for Cleopatra are of two types. Written evidence comes from several ancient accounts, the main ones being that of Dio Cassius in his *Roman History* and that of the historian Plutarch in his *Life of Mark Antony*. There is also a wealth of archaeological evidence, in Rome and in Egypt especially, but also in other outposts of the empire. Also important are inscriptions and coinage, which provide valuable portraiture and other information.

GLOSSARY

consul The title given to a very senior Roman magistrate, a man who had reached the top of the *cursus honorum*. There were always two consuls chosen at any one time, in theory so one could overrule the other. The office is the equivalent in modern-day terms of a prime minister or president. A consul could serve for one year in his post and then often undertook a proconsulship, such as the governorship of a province, which could last for five more years.

dynasty A period of rule where the kings and queens of a land all come from within one family. The dynasty of the Ptolemies lasted in Egypt from 323 BC to 30 BC.

eunuch A castrated male. The Ptolemies often employed eunuchs in top governmental positions, out of fear that their authority would be challenged if their ministers could rear children of their own.

Forum The center of Rome. It consisted of many public buildings, including temples, shops, and law courts.

freedman A person who had once been a slave but was then released from this condition. Freedmen often continued to maintain a social and business relationship with their ex-masters and, in particular, freedmen were often employed as trusted individuals by the emperors.

gymnasium An area where athletes would train or perform. The Gymnasium at Alexandria was a huge colonnaded public building.

imperator This title was given to a general who had been victorious in battle. It was later used as a term to indicate the emperor himself.

Macedonia A large area in the north of Greece, extending into the neighboring countries of Yugoslavia and Bulgaria. Its people considered themselves to be Greek, though not all the other Greeks agreed with them. Its foremost king was Alexander the Great, who died in 323 BC after amassing a huge empire.

republic This term is often used of the Roman state, represented by the acronym SPQR, meaning the Senate and People of Rome. After Augustus became the first emperor of Rome, the republic was in effect an empire controlled by one man, but the illusion was maintained that the republic still existed and that the Senate and people were as important as they had always been in Rome's early history. Republic literally means "public thing."

Senate Body of about 600 senior statesmen, whose authority combined with the emperor's. It acted as the lawgiver of Rome and its importance in Roman history cannot be overestimated.

toga A woolen garment worn by Romans. A ceremony took place when a boy reached the age of around fourteen, when he put on a man's toga for the first time—a big event in a young man's life.

tribune An official whose original job had been to defend the ordinary people of Rome from exploitation by the rich and powerful. A tribune had the right of veto to block discussions taking place in government.

triumph A victory parade in which a Roman general would celebrate a victory in war by leading a procession through the streets of Rome. The people of the city would attend in large numbers, and gifts of money or grain would be handed out as part of the event.

triumvirate A group of three men who assumed the rule of the Roman state. The first triumvirate was formed in 60 BC by Pompey the Great, Julius Caesar, and Marcus Licinius Crassus. The second triumvirate was formed in 43 BC by Mark Antony, Octavian, and Marcus Aemilius Lepidus.

FOR MORE INFORMATION

ORGANIZATIONS

American Research Center in Egypt
  (U.S. Office)
Emory University West Campus
1256 Briarcliff Road, NE
Building A, Suite 423W
Atlanta, GA 30306
(404) 712-9854
e-mail: arce@emory.edu

International Association of
  Egyptologists (USA Branch)
Department of Ancient Egyptian,
  Nubian, and Far Eastern Art
Museum of Fine Arts
465 Huntington Avenue
Boston, MA 02115

JOURNALS

Ancient Egypt
Empire House
1 Newton Street
Manchester M1 1HW
England
e-mail: empire@globalnet.co.uk

WEB SITES

Due to the changing nature of Internet links, the Rosen Publishing Group, Inc., has developed an online list of Web sites related to the subject of this book. This site is updated regularly. Please use this link to access the list:

http://www.rosenlinks.com/lae/cleo/

For Further Reading

Cornell, Tim, and John Matthews. *Atlas of the Roman World*. Oxford, England: Phaidon, 1982.

Grant, Michael. *Cleopatra*. London: Phoenix Press, 1972.

Massie, A. *Antony*. London: Hodder and Stoughton, 1997.

Massie, A. *Augustus*. London: Hodder and Stoughton, 1986.

BIBLIOGRAPHY

PRIMARY SOURCES

Dio Cassius. *The Roman History*.
  London: Penguin, 1987.
Plutarch. *Makers of Rome*. London:
  Penguin, 1965.

SECONDARY SOURCES

Cook, S. A., et al. *The Cambridge
  Ancient History Volume X*. Cambridge,
  England: Cambridge University
  Press, 1966.
Holbl, Gunther. *A History of the Ptolemaic
  Empire*. London: Routledge, 2001.
Hughes-Hallett, Lucy. *Cleopatra*.
  London: Pimlico, 1990.
Scullard, Hugh H. *From the Gracchi
  to Nero*. London: Methuen, 1959.
Talbert, Richard J. A. *Atlas of Classical
  History*. London: Routledge, 1985.

Many of these titles are available from:
Teaching Materials and Resource Center
of the American Classical League, Miami
University, Oxford, Ohio 45056
Web site: http://www.aclclassics.org

INDEX

ABOUT THE AUTHOR

Julian Morgan earned his B.A. in Greek studies at Bristol University, England, in 1979. He also earned a master's degree in computers and education at King's College, London, in 1990. He is currently head of classics at Derby Grammar School. Julian has a special interest in software design and has published many programs, including ROMANA and Rome the Eternal City, through his business, J-PROGS. He is a member of the American Classical League's committee on educational computer applications. He is the computing coordinator for the Joint Association of Classical Teaching (JACT) and has a regular column, "Computanda," in their bulletin. He also runs a training business called Medusa, which specializes in helping teachers of classics to use information technology in their teaching.

CREDITS

EDITOR
Jake Goldberg

DESIGN AND LAYOUT
Evelyn Horovicz